* Sing small notes if there are no Baritones.

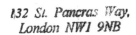

The Camden Music Shop
DOTS

132 St. Pancras Way,
London NW1 9NB

Tel: 020-7482-5424
Fax: 020-7482-5434
E-mail: dot@dotsonline.co.uk
Web: www.dotsonline.co.uk

SA(B) choir & piano

GOSPEL ROCK !

Walk in Jerusalem just like John/By an' by

Just a closer walk with Thee

Daniel was a prayin' man

Arranged by Gwyn Arch

faber Young Voices

FABER *ff* MUSIC

Walk in Jerusalem just like John / By an' by

* First time: Piano only (Intro)

** Throughout the volume, the two notes in this part offer alternatives:
sing the upper, lower or both as you wish.

Just a closer walk with Thee

Daniel was a praying man

* or a few voices

 A collection of four up-beat spirituals in brilliant rock/pop arrangements – *Gospel Rock!* is guaranteed to get audiences' toes tapping!

The *Faber Young Voices* series is devised specifically to address the needs of young or newly-formed choirs looking for easy, yet rewarding new repertoire. Each volume offers:

 A coherent group of pieces to help with concert planning

 Arrangements or original pieces for soprano and alto voices with a manageable piano accompaniment

 An *optional* third line with a narrow range for 'baritone' (newly-changed or unstable voices) or low alto

 Excellent value for money

The series aims to span the fullest possible range of repertoire – both traditional and popular new material from folksongs, spirituals and calypsos to show songs and Christmas favourites.

 Faber Young Voices – the choral series for young choirs!

The Faber Young Voices Series:

Broadway Classics *arranged by Gwyn Arch* ISBN 0-571-51660-2
Christmas Fare *Jane Sebba* ISBN 0-571-51693-9
Classic Pop Ballads *arranged by Gwyn Arch* ISBN 0-571-51639-4
Favourites from Cats *Andrew Lloyd Webber* ISBN 0-571-51614-9
Folksongs from the Wild West *arranged by Gwyn Arch* ISBN 0-571-51533-9
Four Jazz Spirituals *arranged by Gwyn Arch* ISBN 0-571-51523-1
Get on Board! *arranged by Gwyn Arch* ISBN 0-571-51609-2
The Girl from Ipanema *arranged by Gwyn Arch* ISBN 0-571-51850-8
Gospel Rock *arranged by Gwyn Arch* ISBN 0-571-51638-6
Hits from 'Oklahoma' & 'The King & I' *Rodgers & Hammerstein* ISBN 0-571-51745-5
Hits from 'South Pacific' & 'Carousel' *Rodgers & Hammerstein* ISBN 0-571-51746-3
Metropolis *Lin Marsh* ISBN 0-571-52016-2
Pat-a-Pan *arranged by Gwyn Arch* ISBN 0-571-51691-2
Smash Hits for Christmas! *arranged by Gwyn Arch & Robert Winter* ISBN 0-571-51692-0
Songs of the City *arranged by Gwyn Arch* ISBN 0-571-51799-4
Three Caribbean Calypsos *arranged by Peter Gritton* ISBN 0-571-51527-4
Tropical Daydreams *Jane Sebba* ISBN 0-571-51865-6
Walking in the Air & other seasonal songs *Howard Blake* ISBN 0-571-58047-5
West End Showstoppers *arranged by Gwyn Arch* ISBN 0-571-51679-3

ISBN 0-571-51638-6

9 780571 516384

FABER MUSIC · 3 QUEEN SQUARE · LONDON   www.fabermusic.com